YOU AND YOUR TODDLER

Sharing the Developing Years

The Baby Exercise Book

The Baby Exercise Book, Updated & Expanded Edition

YOU AND YOUR TODDLER

Sharing the Developing Years

Dr. Janine Lévy

Preface by Dr. Willibald Nagler

Pantheon Books
New York

LIBRARY OF CONGRESS CATALOGING IN PUBLICATION DATA

Lévy, Janine.
  You and your toddler.

  Translation of L'eveil au monde.
  1. Child development.   2. Children—Management.
I. Title.
HQ769.L39813   649′.1   80-8646
ISBN 0-394-51532-3
ISBN 0-394-74806-9 (pbk.)

A NOTE ON THE ILLUSTRATIONS
Photographs on pages 41, 43, 44, 46, 51, 53 by Alix de Pétigny; photographs on pages 55, 57 by Ville de Paris; photographs on pages 63, 64, 65, 109 by Guy Azémar; photographs on pages 101, 104 by Michel Cambazard; photographs on pages 106, 107, 108, 110, 111 by Marisa Duhalde; all other photographs by Philippe Lévy.

*Parents can give only two things to their children:
Roots and wings.*

PROVERB

CONTENTS

Preface

During the first year of a baby's life, loving care lays the foundation for his coming independence. The pleasurable sensation of the mother's hand and the sound of her guiding voice give the baby confidence in his own world. Until he is at least a year old, the baby is cared for; he plays with the toys offered him and learns to use his arms and legs. There is no doubt that the baby belongs to his mother. After twelve months there is a swift change. All on his own, the baby ventures out. He wants to reach for the toys rather than be handed them. Four-legged locomotion gives way, little by little, to standing up on two feet, and now the baby can reach things more easily. The baby's view of his surroundings changes. The spark of independence has been lit, and it alters the relationship between mother and child. Now, it seems, the mother belongs to the toddler; the parents' role is to watch and guide the surges of his independence. To some measure, the baby makes up his own mind; he plays with the toys within reach, the way he likes to. Regardless of the rules spelled out repeatedly by his mother or father, the baby will make up his own games.

Prior to the age of three or four, the ability to do something with one's extremities, such as crawling back and forth or running up the stairs, is done for the pleasure of the activity itself. The baby doesn't kick a ball for a specific purpose; the kicking itself brings joy. The baby's ability to use his arms and legs in a purposeful way has to be developed. An intentional and smooth motion of an extremity is a very complicated multifactorial event. Through play the toddler practices over and over again how to use his body in an effective and efficient way. For the child, playing is living.

During his toddler years, the baby is testing himself against his environment. This stage is very important. The more the baby is encouraged to explore under the watchful eyes of his parents, and the more familiar he becomes with his surroundings, the safer and more secure he will feel. The feeling of safety and security frees him to continue testing his surroundings and developing mastery of them.

The baby's level of performance, like that of all human beings, is not the same each day. He may try to walk erect up the stairs one day, but find it too cumbersome and not try it again for a few days.

Toddlers often find great pleasure in triggering off events, which may be nerve-racking to their parents. It may be neater and easier for the mother to feed the baby herself, but with utensils the child soon finds an effective way to make a big mess. He gets great joy from plunging recklessly into his food with spoon and fork. Bringing the food to his mouth may not always be his objective. It is important to indulge the child's forays into independence. A few days later, his interest in exploring may turn to something else and his mother can feed him again. The parents have to meet the baby's coming independence with sensitive and flexible guidance.

Different ethnic or social groups often present alternative methods of toilet training. There is no doubt that parents should attempt to explain to their child why he should use the potty or the toilet. I don't know of any infallible method of toilet training. The success stories that are proudly exchanged among mothers may be due to correct timing. Mother nature is a powerful force. I think the best method is to guide the baby but not to force him to do anything for which he is not yet ready.

At the toddler stage, the child may also acquire habits that are very important for success later in life. If he starts a project, his parents should let him pursue it fully until he is satisfied with its completion. In this way the child will learn that any achievement comes about step by step. If his parents interrupt him because they don't think that the task makes any sense or because it is taking up too much time, the child may become very angry and confused. Time does not mean anything to a child; it is something that his parents invented. It is very precious to a child to learn concentration. And this time is the only time in his life when he can do it without restrictions. There is no school, no specific task to do; life is play. How wonderful it is to see a child engrossed in some activity and oblivious to his environment! What an important habit to develop for success in the future!

In contemporary times, mothers and fathers may work and the child may be cared for by a nanny. Despite this, parents should spend a few minutes with their toddler at bedtime. Often, bedtime brings feelings of insecurity for babies. They may feel that they are being excluded from activities that are still going on. In some way, fathers and mothers should point out that they too have to go to bed to get ready for the next day. The toddler should feel that he takes part in the day-and-night rhythm of the grownups.

This excellent book is an extension of Dr. Janine Lévy's earlier book, *The Baby Exercise Book.* In *You and Your Toddler,* Dr. Lévy provides parents with helpful advice on how to deal with their toddler and how to understand the fascinating stages of his development.

—Dr. Willibald Nagler
November 1980

Acknowledgments

I express my gratitude to all those who collaborated from near and far on this work. Without their friendship and help there would have been no book to thank them for. They are:

Jeanine Feller, who knew how to interpret and sharpen my thoughts.
Danielle Rapaport, whose insight into the development of infants helped me enormously.
Dr. Guy Azémar, who gave me the benefit of his teaching experiences and research.
Adolfo Reisin, whose extensive musical background and valuable assistance were very important.
The entire group of my collaborators and the children and personnel of the nurseries.
Julien and his mother, who gave help generously.
My son, Philippe, for the keen photographic sensibility which helped make this book what it is.

LAYING THE FOUNDATIONS

This book follows an earlier work, *The Baby Exercise Book*, in which I presented to parents a technique of exercising that can accompany and facilitate their infant's motor development. The idea was based on my experience with physical therapy for handicapped children. I had noticed that the exercises these babies required—exercises which were regularly performed at home, under the parents' guidance—greatly enhanced the mother–child relationship. But such exercises should certainly not be limited to handicapped children, for they can contribute to the physical development of any child, to his awakening consciousness, to the quality of his relationship with his parents and the outside world. In this way, parents have learned to "awaken" their children through a whole series of progressive exercises.

In this second book I have extended my study to address the needs of toddlers and their parents without leaving the field of psychomotor development, which is my area of expertise. The very word *psychomotor* stresses the simultaneous awakening and development of the child's mind and body through the constant interaction of the two. Psychomotor development is one process. The child's body and mobility are his means of expression during that crucial period from birth to age three. In other words, the baby doesn't *have* a body, he *is* his body, and his entire awakening is experienced through his body. The needs he experiences, the desires he expresses, his mother's responses to his demands and the pleasure that results from her responses, the communication that is established—all are experienced through his body. It is a *body of relationships*.

Three years to build a life

Everything begins with the first day, indeed the very moment of birth, when the new being is greeted on the threshold of its great new adventure.

Mother leaves the hospital with a small "bundle" in her arms, but all too often without proper instructions for its "care and maintenance." This little bundle is a human being, which can already feel and react. And a few rules of hygiene and a prescribed diet are not enough to ensure its best development. It needs awestruck tender looks . . . and, most of all,

great respect. This child whom you hoped for and awaited so eagerly—the most wonderful gift you can give him, from the very first day, is to enter into communication with him. If he is listened to, he in turn will hear and respond. He must be allowed to become himself, with his own tastes, temperament, and personality—a unique being who resembles only himself. In these first three important years, parents lay the necessary foundations to help their child develop. It is a precious and irreplaceable time for both parent and child, for it will establish the framework for his entire life.

This period may seem lengthy to young parents, because it brings with it a large share of restriction and fatigue: so many hours and days of repetitive tasks, of rather monotonous routine! Yet it is a period that requires a lot

of careful attention. This is not lost time, but precious time that has been gained—an impressive investment in the future if one just knows how to take the time to experience it fully. These are brief moments that will never return; this is when the child awakens to the world.

A language to learn

How should this attention be bestowed? Primarily in response to the baby's needs: to be fed, cared for, loved—needs that he expresses in his own individual fashion. Attentive parents quickly learn to distinguish hungry crying from angry crying. The child's refusal to eat is a signal to alert parents, as are his obvious contentment, his peaceful sleep, his cooperation and pleasure in feeding, in being changed, and in being put back to bed. The communication that develops between this tiny being and the person who cares for him is a language, and like any language it involves a mutual give-and-take. If the relationship is a good one, every aspect of daily life will be enriched by it: how the child is approached, held, changed, washed, fed, spoken to, acknowledged, and considered.

A pact that must be made

This is a delicate subject. Being lovingly attentive to wishes that your baby expresses and interpreting the language of his behavior does not mean becoming his slave. Contact with reality includes meeting obstacles. For a child these are supports necessary to the building of his character, and they give structure to his entire development. There is a way to respond sympathetically to your child while remaining firm and refusing to let yourself be devoured by him. I do not mean authoritarianism, but a kind of reciprocal agreement that develops rather quickly and that I refer to as the "pact." There is an art to being moderately permissive without being lax, to knowing just how far to go.

Making experiences possible

A child moves from one stage to the next, gradually increasing his awareness of the world around him and growing in his motor ability. He overcomes the first major obstacle on the road to autonomy when he passes through the decisive stage known as the *motor explosion,* which I will discuss later. Your attitude when he reaches that stage should be to allow him to experience as much as possible—

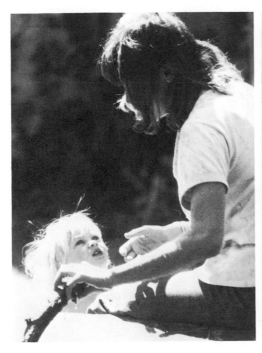

but again without becoming a slave to his whims. Children can become cranky or even tyrannical if they are not allowed to fully investigate things that interest them, or to carry out their wishes. A frequently thwarted child will often become a constantly demanding one. But if you let a baby live through his experiences without interrupting him, he will be a happy and alert child. Of course you may intervene if he is in danger of hurting himself, but you should do it as a stake supports a plant—without crushing it. Parents well versed in this technique will soon observe that a child who is not systematically thwarted takes only progressively manageable risks.

Your relationship will be composed of a constant give-and-take, a dialogue going back and forth between the child's expressed (and satisfied) needs and the limits set by your attitude and voice. The child who has in this way been encouraged and given a sense of security, whose own rhythms have been respected, who has been allowed to experience his motor capabilities to their fullest, will in later life

know how to amuse himself and make his own decisions without anxiety. He will have been encouraged in the acquisition of his own independence.

"I am his mother," not "he is my child"

The former attitude is the opposite of possessiveness. A child is not the property of his parents, even though a mother will sometimes think in terms of "my child, the baby *I* made, who is my posterity and who belongs to me." But if the mother spoke of her child differently, saying "I am his mother," she would not imply ownership of him, but instead a

unique and privileged relationship. Moreover, the words *I am* express the mother's right to her own existence, whereas the child-king or child-tyrant does not allow his mother a truly independent existence.

A shared pleasure

Giving a child the best of oneself has always been a sign of devotion and sacrifice but rarely one of pleasure. However, in a non-possessive relationship there is a strong bond of pleasure between mother and child: the pleasure that is shared at each discovery, at every bit of progress that is made. Physical contact and sensory interaction prolong the intimate relationship that was begun in pregnancy. The mother continues to carry the child as she watches over its progress toward autonomy. Throughout the entire course of the first three years a joyful bond is being forged. This is a long and fascinating adventure.

THE MOTOR
EXPLOSION

It was summertime. The little girl was walking beside me in the flower-filled garden, the belt of my dress grasped firmly in her hand. Then the support she thought she had been dependent on was only a bit of cloth in her hand, and she wasn't even aware of the fact. Suddenly she had been attracted by a gaily colored butterfly poised on a flower, and she tried to seize it. The butterfly took flight but the little girl, too, had been set free, because for the first time she was walking on her own. And she had been motivated by the bright butterfly, not by me!

Demystifying the first steps
I tell this story for a reason. I would somehow

like to "demystify" the child's first steps, make them seem commonplace, just one integrated part of the whole vital process of good motor development. But, you may object, certainly there's a V-Day of walking, and that day is an emotional and joyful one for parents. Doesn't it signal the beginning of the child's independence? Isn't it the sign of an irreversible victory?

Of course it marks a decisive stage in the child's achievement of independence, but it is one that must be reached naturally, when the child herself wants to do so. The age at which a child begins to walk is of little importance. What counts is *how* it happens. Was she forced into it by parents who stood her against a wall and then coaxed her to come into their outstretched arms as she struggled to overcome her fear and take the risk, their pleading voices urging "Come on! Come on!"? If that was the case, she will have done it to please them, and, one might say, without any great personal conviction. Can you imagine a mountain climber who is forced to scale a peak that

he feels is beyond his capabilities? How many parents set on her feet again the child who has fallen after taking three steps? It is as if they want to urge her to keep trying, not to stop while she is making such wonderful progress. Such behavior makes me want to cry out, "Leave that child alone!" She'll get up again all by herself when she's good and ready to. But it is equally wrong to fearfully restrict the child who, out of her own desires, is boldly lunging along from obstacle to obstacle. Parents, prepare yourselves to face the arrival of the motor explosion!

An explosion is a sudden (and sometimes devastating) occurrence, but it is the culmination of a whole process of development. Buds burst open in spring only after their long winter's sleep, and the eruption of a volcano is the culmination of preceding internal activity. Like a

bud or a volcano, the small child who has just taken her first step is proving that she has achieved a certain level of development, a process that really started much earlier.

The discovery of the body

At the the age of two or three months, an infant stubbornly tries to turn over onto her back after having been placed on her stomach; then she grasps exploringly into the air around her and seizes objects; later she crawls, sits up; finally she stands up. The baby has mastered all the stages of her normal motor development. What is the role of the parents in this development? Their primary role is as spectators. But they are also allies in that they make it possible for her to have new experiences and to take risks in an environment of security and love.

A child's motor abilities can be seen from the moment of birth. A newborn infant placed on her mother's stomach will wriggle to the breast and begin to nurse. This is called the entrenchment reflex. But not all children can benefit from this immediate relationship, because most births today are under rigid medical supervision and the child is quickly separated from her mother. The mother will have to discover for herself that the small bundle placed in her arms when she leaves the hospital is something other than a few pounds of squalling flesh that she must feed and keep clean; it is a living and active body, the body of a child.

It is primarily through sensory contact, as when bathing or taking care of the child, that adults can encourage the first signs of the baby's motor development. For example, when you are changing a baby you can avoid the usual choppy gestures of flipping her over and back, like a pancake. Instead try pausing between gentle turning motions that encourage her to participate in what is going on. In so doing you are not going to turn her into an acrobat, or even a child who is "advanced for her age." She would certainly have discovered the new movements for herself in the normal course of her development. But by constantly

watching over and encouraging her progress without trying to anticipate or rush it, the parent helps make the child aware that her body exists and that she can be happy in and through her body.

The joy of walking

There is no doubt that the first astronaut to set foot on the moon experienced a moment of intense jubilation. Every child lives through a similar moment when she can first take a step without anyone's help. Walking on two feet is, after all, a very useful means for exploring the unknown. Of course walking on all fours wasn't bad either, for even that marked notable progress over the crawling that preceded it.

In any case, being able to move standing up is a magnificent discovery. The child can finally see what is going on at a normal height, without being reduced to exploring the underside of tables; she can nimbly seize a desired object without having to beg for it; and, best of all, she can practice that wonderful new exercise: walking for walking's sake. She propels herself back and forth, from object to object, steadily gaining confidence; now she walks faster, up and down the room, going sideways and turning, coming back to her starting point again— the day isn't long enough for all of it!

If you watch the constant activity of a child who is just beginning to walk, you will see that she is completely absorbed in her movements. Everything is acquired in successive stages, always according to the same formula: She explores a possibility, makes her first groping attempts, stubbornly repeats them un-

til at last she succeeds. Once she has done so she seems to lose interest, and sets forth on new explorations. The thrill is in the pleasure of discovery. She will attempt to overcome, one by one, the obstacles in her path. For her it is really a field of combat. This jubilant time marks a turning point in the parent–child relationship. It is a privileged period of joy and shared pleasures: for the child, the pleasure of walking and of her conquests; for the parent, the pleasure in being able to observe the child's daily progress, her growing independence, and her reaching an important stage in her development. But it is normal for the parent to experience mixed emotions at this time. An ounce of regret accompanies the pride in seeing the child walk, for it marks the end of an era. She is no longer the helpless infant

completely dependent on her parents for every little thing. Every bit of progress carries her farther away from that total dependence. It is time for the parent to begin letting go. But that detachment should be mixed with joy. "My" child is really "that" child, who was born not to satisfy *me* but to live her own life. A new period is beginning and the relationship will be entirely different. Through their attitude and behavior, parents will enable the child to become herself. If they have been overly possessive up until now, this is the time to forge a different kind of bond.

The motor explosion and the parent–child pact

Once a child can walk there's no limiting her

activity. This is the motor explosion, an exhausting period for parents who dread its onslaught much as they would a hurricane. But one would no more keep a child from exploratory activities than one would gag someone whose constant chatter was irritating! In any case, you should realize that this phase will not last forever. Once the child has confronted obstacles and tested her capabilities and her limits she will go on, of her own accord, to other activities for other purposes.

In the meantime her ambition increases daily. As she goes from victory to victory she will inevitably confront the forbidden. What will happen then? She cautiously climbs one step, then a second one. But if she climbs ten, how will she get back down? She's learning how to open a closet door, but will you let her pull out the dishes inside, or mix the salt with the pepper? Why not? It's not really a terribly important issue, but here's where your own personal tolerance threshold comes in, and that

pact that will be so important to future relations between you. Implicit in the pact is a message that will settle (or prevent) many future arguments: "I will respect you, and you will respect me! Agreed?" I cannot give a more detailed description of the exact terms of the pact. Each father and mother must judge for themselves how far they will go in accepting or rejecting an activity that one person will find unbearable, another amusing. In short, everyone should be able to live his or her own life without impinging on other people's rights. A parent can be nondirective and still impose a certain number of restrictions that the child must respect. But it is essential that both parents agree on what these are, that they not be simply reflections of a passing mood. This would only disconcert the child, causing her to question the wisdom of her parents.

You will quickly realize that there need not be many of these restrictions, though some are es-

sential to give the child the foundation she needs to build upon.

Managing one's space

Two things usually worry parents when their child first begins to walk: their concern for their child's safety and their concern for their own peace of mind. The latter includes the perfectly legitimate desire not to see belongings strewn around, knickknacks broken, papers crumpled, and closets emptied when they are within the reach of rummaging little hands.

Of course the child's safety is of prime concern. To ensure it one must figure out what the real risks are and give some thought to preventing them. Some obvious examples of dangers are a balcony without a proper railing, a window that the child can easily get to by climbing on a chair, scissors or pins within the child's reach, a pot of boiling water whose handle is sticking out, and unprotected electrical outlets. The younger a child is when she begins to walk, the more careful you will have

to be, keeping a watchful eye on her and removing anything that might be dangerous.

This is a trying period. The child seems to be into everything. Indeed, she has a real need to touch things in order to judge their consistency, how resistant they are, and to build her own store of knowledge. How can she be stopped without hindering her progress? Here's where the pact mentioned earlier comes in. There are objects that must never be touched—and the child will quickly identify them by the tone of her parent's voice as she gets near them! Most other objects will fall into a neutral category. Everything will depend on how they are used, and learning to use them will become part of the child's education. "If I take my child out of the playpen, she'll break all the knickknacks on the table—and I like them," says one mother. Fine. She should let the child run around the room and put the knickknacks in the playpen! If she prefers leaving them on the table, the child must spend a longer time in the playpen, until she is famil-

iar with the pact and knows not to touch forbidden things.

The security–risk balance

The security–risk balance is a fundamental equilibrium and an idea that I will often return to in this book. Its primary meaning is that one can only take risks according to one's capabilities, and a child's capabilities vary according to her progress. Parents should let their young children decide for themselves how much they are going to attempt, find their own supports, and get out of difficult situations by themselves. Parents should not keep saying "Watch out," but instead should let the child herself become watchful, attentive to her own safety and aware of the risks she is taking.

A staircase might be considered dangerous for a child who is beginning to walk. It is, however, a wonderful game for the child to keep climbing up and coming back down the same one or two steps. But coming home from the store, the child has to put this same new ability to work, and not make Mommy carry her. In this case the parent–child pact consists of, on the one hand, Mother's patient supervision of the activity the child enjoys—making time for it whenever she can, without hurrying the child, and letting her follow her own rhythms—and on the other hand the child's growing ability to accept responsibility as little by little she learns to put her activity to practical use. "You want to climb the stairs? Good girl. Mommy's right here waiting for you."

Of course, there are daredevil children and timid children—but many fewer daredevils than you might think. Timid children are often those who have been pushed into activities they were not ready for: the child who is placed at the top of a sliding board and told "I'll wait for you down in front," when she expressed no desire to go on it; the child who harbors the painful memory of a failure. Sooner or later she will return to the activity of her own accord, when she is ready for it, if she is allowed to regain her confidence without being forced to compete with herself. Some children begin to walk precociously, but for a short time will revert to hanging onto Mommy's skirt because they again feel a great need for security and dependence.

This happens because the security–risk balance involves another dimension, the entire emotional context of the child. Her security is not guaranteed simply by removing from her field of exploration things that can harm her physically. Also essential to the child's sense of security are her parents' presence, their loving looks, the warmth of their arms where she can take refuge. This is the emotional fuel that each child seeks even before she knows how to ask for it.

The child's psychomotor progression occurs as a series of apprenticeships, a kind of visual navigation between trial and error by a thousand attempts and eventual successes. The parents' irreplaceable role is to be attentively present during this crucial stage of a young child's motor development.

DAILY GESTURES

Little by little the child discovers and explores his body and learns to master his motor functions. A whole universe is his to be acquired. The development of the healthy child occurs in the course of a daily life that has certain controlling rhythms: eating, sleeping, playing, dirtying himself, getting washed, cementing relationships with his parents and the outside world. His relationships are in fact determined by his becoming familiar with daily rhythms that allow him to develop, to get his bearings, and to grow—in both the literal and figurative senses of that word.

The first relationship, or the pleasure in feeding

In his mother's womb the baby is fed continuously. After birth he suddenly experiences for the first time a painful sensation—hunger. A vital cycle is about to be established in an essentially emotional context: pleasure of feeding/displeasure of hunger. In the first moments of life, being fed usually means being placed at the mother's breast, experiencing the well-being of bodily contact with the mother (from whom the child is not yet completely separate). Many pediatricians today believe that breast feeding should begin immediately after birth. We have already seen that the newborn infant placed on his mother's stomach will move instinctively toward her breast. This first motor reflex is linked with olfaction—for a long time the infant will be able to recognize his mother's odor—and already constitutes the beginning of the important emotional relationship that will be formed between them.

The mother–child relationship is based primarily on feeding. Nothing is more satisfying to a mother than seeing her child eat well. He must do so in order to gain weight, to grow, to develop. But there is another aspect to this that I think is as important as the weight gain:

the pleasure of feeding. While the child's eating certainly pleases his mother, he himself takes pleasure in it because the sensation of appeased hunger bestows on him a well-being that is also linked with other pleasant sensations: the warmth of the arms that are holding him, the familiar odor of his mother, the tenderness she shows as she holds him close to her, whether she is nursing him or giving him a bottle. Well-being, tenderness, security—feeding means all of these, and they are just as important as the physical contribution that is necessary to growth.

But let the child refuse to eat and the shared pleasure threatens to turn into a disaster scene. Baby rejects the nipple, he spits up his cereal. At last he gives in, swallowing everything—and then vomits. His parents see the horizon darkening, and anxiety is born. The good relationship that had been formed begins to deteriorate. But there is one factor that all parents should be aware of. A child will not let himself die of hunger, except in the very rare case of a severe psychiatric problem that would also manifest itself in many other symptoms. Par-

ents must remember that a child's hunger does not automatically obey their wishes or respond to their pleas. As he grows, the child (like an adult) will come to hate one food and adore another. New tastes surprise him, and occasionally he will need time to get used to them. In this he is already showing that he is an individual human being, worthy of attention, not some small animal that just has to be stuffed with food. He is one individual child, and not another one. It is his *right* to be less hungry today than he was yesterday.

Is it necessary for a child to learn to eat everything? The sense of taste begins to form in early infancy, and it is a good idea to have your child try many different kinds of foods very early on. But you should do so without insisting or making scenes. Appetite must be seen in relation to an entire psychological context. Not just the food itself, but the entire circumstances surrounding feeding at any given moment can increase or decrease appetite. A truly attentive mother realizes this and knows just how far she can go in making her child eat. An equilibrium must be found every day for each child.

In feeding your child you must know how to insist just a little bit, taking enough time for the child to eat according to his own rhythm, without hurrying. No matter what you were made to do, you should not allow yourself to force your child to always finish everything on his plate. But this does not mean you should indulge a child who demands cookies and candy, and then cannot eat his regular food.

Why will a mother let her child gorge himself on cookies? Perhaps simply for the sake of peace. But then she should not be surprised if the child is no longer hungry, or penalize him for his loss of appetite. After all, coherence is part of the parent–child pact.

Parents tend to worry more about a lack of appetite in their child than they do about overeating. But if a child takes refuge in the satisfaction food brings him, is that a healthier sign than if from time to time he is not hungry? His overeating may betray a certain need that his parents should try to identify. It may be a sign of an emotional deprivation that the child is compensating for in his own way.

The time will arrive when the child wants to feed himself, inaugurating a new stage in the parent–child relationship and a new experience to be lived through. What is really going on? The child is beginning to be interested in something other than the pleasure of taste.

Now before he eats what he sees on his plate he wants to touch it, smell it, feel it with his hands. At the same time he discovers the use of the spoon. He can now become the instigator of all the back-and-forth activity from plate to mouth that he used to submit to passively. His clumsy little hands are active, plunging recklessly into his food. But most likely once he has explored this new activity he will lose interest in it and prefer the simple solution, which was letting himself be fed. This is not a step backward, but a temporary halt if he has found something new to attract his interest. And all along his mother is there, ever watchful, following each stage without trying to rush him, knowing how to impose necessary

restrictions ("You don't throw cereal at Mommy!") without overdoing them.

Mealtime: an inauguration into family life

The meals which set the rhythm of daily life also have an important social and familial function. Of course we eat to live, but also to meet, to get together for a pleasant occasion. A family meal is a time for relaxing, for conversation; a time when we share not only bread but also ideas and the events of the day. The child should become a part of this quite early, for it is the best way to stimulate his appetite and his mind at the same time. If the grownups of the family eat too late for him to share the evening meal with them, he should at least be able to eat a leisurely meal in the kitchen, where he can be taught the colors and names of vegetables and foods as they are being prepared.

The more smoothly meals are integrated into the rest of the child's life, the better off he will be. Eating should contribute to his psychic development as well as to his growth in size and weight.

Sleep is also a pleasure

Isn't it obvious that sleep is a pleasant pastime? Then why is a child punished by being sent to bed? "If you don't finish your soup you're going straight to bed!" threatens a parent—and then he wonders why the child so often balks at bedtime. Bed has become synonymous with punishment, or with banishment by a tired parent who has had a long day and just wants a little peace and quiet. This is a classic scene, and the child will find a hundred excuses to remain with the rest of the family as night falls: He's thirsty, he needs the potty, he wants his teddy bear—anything but to go to sleep.

What kind of pact can be made in this case? Again, agreeing to respect one another: "We'll play with you a little longer. This is your time." Then: "Now you're going to bed. This is our time."

Children find nighttime mysterious. A child rarely sees his parents sleeping and he imagines that he is being excluded from a family activity that is taking place without him, once the adults have sent him to bed. Why not explain to your child early on that Mommy and Daddy will be going to bed too, but first they have work to finish, and want to spend some time together? You must always explain things to your child, and you should try to spend at least a little time with him in the evening so he can go to bed happy and relaxed, if possible having spent time with both parents.

Alas, nighttime is not always restful for parents. There are cries of hunger from the newborn child, nightmares, the fevers of childhood illnesses. The baby cries, wants to be held, then wants to be comforted in his parents' bed. There is no doubt that you can calm a child by taking him into your bed, but you are also encouraging one of the worst habits you can instill in him. He soon won't be able to give it up, and you won't know how to break him of it. A much better strategy is for you to remain quietly by him until he goes back to sleep, even if you yourself are exhausted and dread the idea of facing tomorrow after having spent a sleepless night.

Raising a child imposes a certain number of restrictions on your life, and you will encounter some every day. Parent–child relations are not always idyllic: Nerves get frazzled, tiredness becomes exhaustion. But you must remember to try not to let things upset you too much. This phase will pass quickly—even too quickly. The child who gets everything from you now is going to grow, to become more independent. Parents can best contribute to that process by treating the child as an equal (at his own level, of course), a separate human being who is on the way to becoming self-possessed and fully responsible for his actions. That is one of the best gifts parents can give him.

Toilet training

"You must go in the potty to please Mommy." That's what the child is told. But then why

does Mommy immediately throw away what she's just been given? Grownups are so inconsistent!

Going in the potty because it's cleaner to do so is a much more sophisticated personal concept. But what is cleanliness? It is purely subjective. There are people who are maniacs for order, and there are disorderly people.

If there is one area that should be played down in daily life, it is this one. Fortunately, disposable diapers, one of the great inventions of our century, have greatly simplified life for parents.

In any case, one thing is certain: The child will become toilet trained when he wants to. Before he is eighteen months to two years old, it is futile even to seriously attempt to train him. Never mind the grandmothers and neighbors who have "infallible methods." Most early "successes" are due to chance, not to the child's will. It is absolutely essential that you not try to push your child in this area, that you wait until the child has reached the proper stage in his neurological and motor development, and in his ability to understand what is required of him.

PLAY AS
CREATIVE ACTIVITY

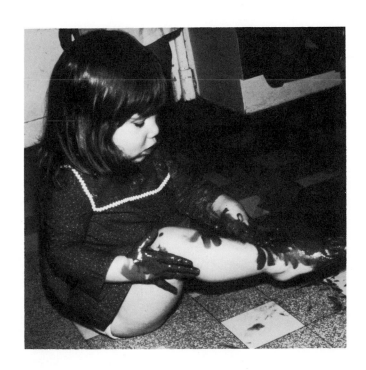

For the child, playing is living. It is a vital function (animals play, too) as necessary as sleep or food. A child who did not play would be psychologically dead. It is through play that the child will learn many important things, constantly confronting the reality of her environment and her own limitations—of life, in short. But play is a very special kind of learning, for it is accomplished pleasurably and pursued through the child's own initiative. It is her creation, in the strongest sense of the word.

The child's first plaything is her own body. The infant's awakening unfolds in her discovery of herself, from head to toe. She'll spend hours just playing with her own hands, exploring her entire body. When she gurgles at the joy of having caught hold of her feet, she has reached a new level of development and her pleasure bears witness to it: She has just perceived that the foot and the hand that is holding it are *hers*. Mommy's hand is not part of her. The me and the non-me are dissociated; the child's mental universe is taking form. Then, when she begins to walk, at the height of her motor explosion, the child moves beyond the pleasure of discovering her body. Other, equally fascinating discoveries await her.

The jubilation of walking is followed by the child's pleasure in her motor abilities, in overcoming the feelings of insecurity and weakness which were her lot until then. Contact with objects allows her to take her own measure. Climbing up on a chair, crawling back and forth under a table—everything she does has a meaning. She is testing herself against difficulties and overcoming them. Motor activity is itself a game, as well as a necessity for good development.

The parents' role during this stage of ceaseless activity that follows the child's mastery of walking is to make the child's experiences possible. It is very important that their attitude be one that allows the child to have her own existence. This attitude had its roots long before, in their desire to have a child. That desire was embodied: the child they hoped for was born.

Parents today can usually plan the birth of their child. They have literally permitted it to exist. But this permission does not stop with conception and the child's development during pregnancy. On the contrary, the adventure is just beginning. This is the basis of an essential attitude that will nourish the child's mental and psychic development throughout the early years of her growth—a welcoming attitude in the face of her innate capabilities and potential creative energy. This energy bubbles forth during her play, the motor activity that is a highly creative and irreplaceable expression of her own personality.

How can you help the child to have new experiences? In several ways: You can organize the space around her; you can let her go to the limits of her own initiative; you can know when to urge on the child who is waiting for

approval before venturing forth to something new. Children often need the approval implicit in an adult's acknowledgment of what they are doing, and the emotional support that bestows security on them.

Organize the space around your child so that it is manageable without your having to impose too many restrictions. Of course these will sometimes be necessary, mainly for circumscribing real dangers that can arise from objects whose injurious nature the child has not yet experienced: the knife that can cut, the iron that will burn, the flame that must not be approached. Be sure to explain the limitation; "no" is part of the parent–child pact, but it must always be logical and comprehensible.

Encouraging the child's initiative also means letting her touch things and giving her things to play with. It does not matter what they are, so long as they provide her with sensory stimulation and are not dangerous. An infant in an empty room can roll around on the ground, suck her thumb, take off her booties and pull on her toes. She cannot climb the walls. Any

object is fine and will become a fascinating toy if it gives rise to seeing, hearing, tasting, smelling, touching, moving, climbing, or exploring. By *toy* here I mean anything that puts the child in touch with daily reality. It is well known that at this age a baby will often remain indifferent to an expensive toy that has been purchased for her but will spend hours pulling around a piece of wood attached to a string, or banging on a pot. Everyday objects are extremely attractive to children, because they want to imitate the gestures they have observed around them. They can also find a multitude of uses for these things. The kitchen pot is always tempting. It can be used in water games. It can be turned into a drum or into a hat. It can be emptied and filled over and over again—outside, with sand; in the house, with grains of rice, marbles, or acorns gathered from the garden—and eventually it will be used for cooking! What matters is less the object itself than the activities it makes possible, for it is through them that the child accumulates experience and develops her knowledge, skills, and personality.

What about "educational" toys? In my opinion they are objects like any others. They may be attractively colored and have practical advantages if they are unbreakable and harmless, but it is up to the child to decide how she wants to use them—without having read the instructions on the box, or knowing which stage of development she is supposed to have reached at her age!

She will indeed reach all stages and make all the requisite progress, but according to her own pace and rhythm. Hers, not her sister's or her cousin's. Whether she spends her days at home or in a child-care center, if she is allowed to explore and make progress at her own rate, without being either rushed or hindered, she will gropingly but fearlessly arrive at the top of her ladder of success. Then she will

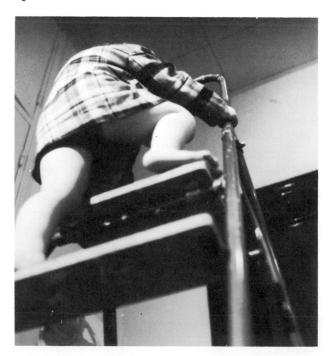

climb it, not for the pleasure of climbing, but for the pleasure of being on top, under Mommy's or Daddy's admiring eye. Later on, when she climbs, it will be to play at being someone or something else. From the motor phase she'll go on to the wonderful age of the imagination.

Allowing the child to experiment and to explore her own initiatives means letting her pursue them *fully*. A child who is constantly reined in and opposed, who can never finish what she starts out to do, risks becoming a dissatisfied adult. Parents are always in a hurry; children at that marvelous age from birth to three, before the restrictions of school begin, have all the time in the world. For them, time is just something invented by grownups. If the child has started to climb up that ladder, or is playing with her blocks, why interrupt her for something unimportant and ruin her concentration? Concentration is a very precious gift. If she is always interrupted she may be lacking in it later on, when as a schoolgirl she tries to do her homework but her mind wanders. Then her parents will be sorry. But how wonderful it is to see a tiny human being engrossed in a task she has set herself. This time of foundations is the preparation for the future—a point that cannot be overemphasized.

From motor activity to creative activity

What does creation mean for the child? The word usually makes us think of prettily colored drawings that adults rave over because they express a kind of creativity whose source is all too quickly exhausted. But creative activity in the sense that I mean covers a much broader field, and is linked to the child's personality. Because she is the person she is, everything she does is a constant act of creation, a *personal* masterpiece—if she is left to her own initiative. From her very first steps and explorations, her motor activity becomes creative activity. That is why it is so important to nurture it. And the child's most important creation is ultimately herself.

A child's activity should occupy a privileged place in the home, in daily life. Very early on, she should be allowed to do things with adults. In the kitchen, you should let her "help" with the baking; in the workshop, let her help with the carpentry. Older children should share some of their clay with her so she can do her own modeling. This is also a good time for teaching the names of the objects she sees and touches. Even if she cannot yet talk, her overall development will benefit from such activities. Remember how the word *language* was defined earlier. More will be said about this subject in the next chapter, but motor ability and language go hand in hand when it's a question of the child's situating herself in space. The game of going *under* the table, of crawling *into* a large box, of throwing a ball *over* her head is a good example of this.

If the child has been allowed to proceed at her own rate and been encouraged in her own initiatives, her physical and motor creativity will one day be transformed into true creativity: graphic, pictorial, or musical. Through the discoveries of play, the child will have attained her first mastery of the universe around her and a satisfying form of personal expression.

VOCAL EXPRESSION, OR ENTRY INTO THE WORLD OF SOUNDS

When the child is born he has already entered into the world of sounds. Today we know that in intrauterine life, inside his mother's womb, the fetus hears sounds, perceives his mother's and father's voices. Then he will hear the sounds spoken at his birth, the first words addressed directly to him. He hears and stores them in his unconscious mind. During his infancy, the role of his parents and of all those around him will be to develop his senses so that he in turn will acquire his own form of vocal expression, the prelude to language and to music.

You may say that music appreciation is easily acquired today. Recordings of the greatest virtuosos are available to everyone; babies can be cradled from the day of birth to the strains of Beethoven's Fifth Symphony or the rhythm of rock and roll. But I'm talking about something else. The latest attitude toward this subject involves a certain modesty on the part of the child's teachers. Instead of imposing sounds on the child, they wait and listen to him. We adults respond to the sounds around us, and the child will do the same. Especially if he has brothers and sisters, he will not grow up in a padded world. Very early he will hear radios, television, the ringing of the telephone. But a child's expression is not something ready-made, or that comes to him from outside. It's

his own individual form of expression, and it includes all the noises he can produce: the noise of his rattle, which he discovers he can start and stop at will; the gurgling sounds he makes during his early months; his first vocalizations that parents so eagerly await, and then repeat back to him.

Letting the child hear himself

Certain misconceptions have to be cleared up right here. At the risk of astonishing many parents, I do not think it is useful to give records to babies. The reasons that prompt parents to do so are theoretically excellent: They want to educate their child's ear with tunes and songs, counting rhymes, and the rounds that were part of their own childhood; to give him entry into a tradition of sound that will gradually lead him to song and language, with good models to follow. All these things can be put to work at a later stage in his own vocal development, but there is a time for everything. Before he can sing "Twinkle, Twinkle, Little Star" he must have heard the sound of his own voice and discovered that he himself is a crea-

tor. He must be the "transmitter," taking an active role, and not the "receiver," passively immobilized in front of his record player.

The role of receiver should be played by the parents. They are the ones who will repeat the sounds made by their child, making them concrete for him and showing him that his sounds exist, that they hear them. The sounds the child makes are his language, and his crying is his vocal expression. Parents can distinguish its nuances; by its tone and cadence it reveals its meaning: angry crying, a cry of appeal, a cry of distress, bored crying. The child emits sounds spontaneously, but if they fall into a vacuum he will not make progress. He needs a live audience that will listen to his sounds, use them, and bounce them back to him. One day the sounds will become language, rhythm, and music. This communication—which is entirely instinctive—gradually becomes a kind of game between parent and child and creates an emotional bond between them. The child who has been heard will have more opportunity to hear himself and to be understood and get along with those around him.

So sound becomes another means of education. Early vocalizations are followed by the discovery of the universe of sounds: the noise made by hitting a bottle or a table with a fork, the noise made by a marble placed inside a bottle, the whooshing sound of sand being poured out. But this kind of education has its restrictions, too. The child has fun rapping on the table while it is being set, but he must stop when meals start; he can tap his clogs on the pavement, but in the house the noise is annoying, and is not allowed. Those are the terms of the unbreakable pact. Moreover, his parents' tone of voice—another sound—suffices to indicate this clearly.

Later he will also learn to listen to "silence." How wonderful it is to discover sounds in nature that can be perceived only if you have learned to stop making noises yourself.

From sound to melody: giving and receiving messages

Little by little the child comes to understand that a sound can have several meanings, depending on its tone, strength, volume, tempo, and rhythm. There is a permissive tone, and a forbidding one that means danger—the frantic "Don't touch!" of the mother whose child is about to stick his fingers into an electric outlet. That tone is different from a playfully forbidding one, or from the one used for "because I am your mother and I say no."

We know that sounds are not neutral. For each of us they are tied to memories, and lead us into a world of symbols. They can create an atmosphere of harmony or one of discord. The ticking of a clock or the sound of a church bell that tells the hours and marks the rhythm of our daily life, familiar voices, the tune played by an ice-cream truck in summer. . . . The child goes to sleep every night listening to the tinkle of his music box or, even better, the melody Mommy softly plays for him on a little xylophone. Can you think of a better way to bring pleasant dreams?

The difference between sound and music is only one of degree. One day the child will joyfully reach the world of music, moving from expressing himself with any kinds of noises he can make to true musical and even instrumental expression—but with a real instrument, not a tinny little piano that can ruin his ear! Quite early you should put different kinds of instruments at his disposal so he can use them, not to "make noise" but as another language. He

will learn that he can make the instrument communicate a message, and he will derive great pleasure from it. How wonderful it is to see a child dancing to music he's making himself, drawing others into the dance!

And language?

Many parents worry when their child has not yet started to talk. After the walking phase, the talking phase is often anxiously awaited. But there is nothing that varies more from child to child than the acquisition of speech. A whole set of conditions—his desire to talk, his opportunities, the environment—plays a role in it. For certain children, communication with the mother has been so intense—although it is only a matter of looks and a kind of complicity—that the child has always felt understood and does not experience the need to express himself otherwise. For other children, who have not been spoken to often enough, words remain an alien universe, and they learn to make themselves understood through mimicry.

But the child who was listened to when he first started making noises will *want* to speak. Because he was responded to, he in turn will answer. First he will repeat the words he hears, and then he will be able to sing with other children. His voice has been heard and he hears those of others; he passes from his individual universe to a collective universe, eventually to that of nursery school and other group functions. He will be more easily integrated into it if he has first been encouraged to exist as an individual and unique human being.

WATER: A SPECIAL
WAY OF LEARNING

It's not really anything new—newspapers and magazines have written articles about it—but it hasn't yet become a common practice: taking babies from the age of three or four months on to a pool and putting them in the water. These children have been described as "swimming babies," as though the goal were to begin preparing them at that tender age for future Olympic performances. But the experiment has an entirely different purpose.

There the babies are, floating in the water, lying or seated on foam-rubber mats, kicking and splashing with their hands and feet, or carefully filling and emptying their little buckets, playing as they would on the mat in their playpen. Some of them paddle around by themselves, a small life preserver around their tummy or arms, and head toward an object that has caught their attention—or toward their parents, who are in the water with them. In fact there are fathers and mothers around them, and a few older children jumping into the water from the side of the pool. There is hardly any screaming or crying, but an atmosphere of gaiety and well-being. This unusual scene quickly comes to seem completely natural to someone seeing it for the first time. Something unexpected and harmonious is happening, and it is a delight to watch. To say that this is a learning experience seems almost inappropriate. More striking is the pleasure shared by parents and children, the joy the parents experience as they watch their baby. And that is just the point of the experiment: The shared pleasure and the harmony are the very symbol of the relationship that should exist between parents and their young child. The mother–child or father–child pair—or, better yet, the father–mother–child triad—is experiencing a moment of great happiness.

Why give water a special place in the child's life? In our society water has a reputation as a dangerous medium, and it's certainly true that it would be foolish to leave the child in the water without surveillance. But for the infant who has not yet learned to crawl or walk, water can provide a unique opportunity for in-

dependent mobility; and at such a young age, children will not have developed the fear of water, which often becomes an impediment later on. This pool session with parents is really a lesson in conduct: for the parents, learning how to behave with the child; for the child, learning to be independent.

How are parents going to behave when they see their very young child placed in a "dangerous" situation? Their behavior is revealing. For several weeks a camera followed the progress in the water of two babies and their parents. The first time little Delphine was filmed, the cameraman focused the camera on the baby, who was in the water on a flexible mat. But what showed up when the film was projected? The child's face was constantly hidden from view by four hands moving frantically around her—touching her, holding her back, clutching her at every slightest movement she attempted to make. It was a real four-hand ballet (there would have been more had it been possible!), four frightened, grabbing hands whose nervousness was contagious. In fact, Delphine

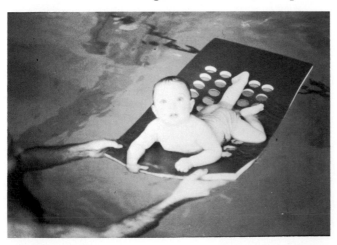

had been perfectly happy the first time she was placed in the water, but it didn't take long for her to become afraid; after that, it took several months for her to feel at ease again.

There is also a film that shows another child, Anne, on her mat. She is the same age as Delphine, but she is calm and relaxed in the water. There is no sign of hands around her. Then the camera zooms out and we see her admiring parents nearby. They are close enough for the child to be reassured by their presence, but they do not interfere with her movements. The water is carrying the baby, but at one point she makes a sudden movement and slides off the mat, plunging into the water. Then we see her father's large hand slowly reach out and gently scoop her out of the water to put her back on the mat. There has not been a trace of panic:

Anne could feel the movement with her body; she felt herself being buoyed up by the water, and her father assisted that movement. Daddy and Mommy are there; the water is good. Anne is not afraid.

If, on the other hand, one of the parents quickly snatched back the child who had slid off the mat and pressed her to him, he would immediately communicate his fear to her (if only by the manner in which she was seized).

Thus we can see that water plays a very revealing role here. Because the situation involves risk, behavior is amplified in such a way that the symbolism of the relationship can be grasped. Not only fear and anxiety, but also authoritarianism and the tendency to be domineering are exposed, as are their opposites—calm, benevolence, confidence in the child's abilities, and admiration on her behalf. Are the parents going to allow their child to attain independence? Or are they going to constantly interfere with her, projecting their own fears onto the child? These sessions in the pool, as

well as providing pleasure and a sense of admiration in parents who see their child so free and relaxed in the water, improve the parent–child relationship, allowing anxiety to come to light and be dispelled.

As I suggested earlier, learning to swim is not the main point at all. In any event, the child who has been given confidence will gradually start moving around by herself and head toward her parents. There is no need to give her a model, to say, "Look at me! Do what I'm doing!" That would only curb her spontaneity. She needs no model to show her how to paddle in the water with all the strength her little legs can manage. In any case, the best models are other children, her equals, who are in the same situation and whose presence stimulates her. The baby will also try to grab a big ball floating in front of her, which constantly bobs away as she tries to approach it. To reach it she will have to correct her movements, veering to the right or to the left. Can one imagine a better lesson in motor skills?

And so she learns, gropingly, by a steady series of trials and errors until her goal is reached. Success will eventually crown the efforts of the person who is truly motivated by a goal, whatever that may be. That is true in any learning situation, and water here is only one example of it—albeit a special example, for it allows more flexibility, completely surrounds the child, carries her, and keeps her from holding on. For the experience to be a positive one, it must take place in an atmosphere of emotional security. What parents contribute is not a model, but the warmth of their presence and of their loving glances.

"Surprise me!" is what the parents' delighted looks seem to say. Daddy's or Mommy's hand is there as an assurance of safety, even if it never intervenes. And the water itself is reassuring, holding the child afloat.

Even when the pool sessions have ended, the discoveries that have been made together and the joy in the new relationship that has been established remain to be explored. Parents must constantly seek to maintain an equilibrium between the risks their child can reasonably take, without always being hampered in her initiatives, and the security she needs—the loving presence and watchfulness of an adult. It is in the security–risk balance that the art of teaching a child resides.

THE CITY CHILD

What place does the city child occupy in our society? He's given a lot of space in advertisements for products, but we don't make much room for him in the streets. If babies' sweet faces and plump little bodies are shown in television commercials and magazine ads, it's because the infant is already a consumer. Disposable diapers, folding carriages, commercial baby foods, "educational" toys, miniature blue jeans, tiny jogger's outfits and college sweatshirts—all are available for babies.

But just let the child who has been given all these things try to disturb his parents, and interfere with their life style!

Child-oriented products are more or less useful, and many of them unquestionably simplify a mother's life, but they really serve to obscure the true situation. Children in our cities today are overburdened with gadgets, but they are deprived of certain essential benefits: clean air, space to run around and play in, grass to frolic on, and time that their parents can devote to them.

Mothers who stay at home and should be able to spend time with their children instead find their days constantly taken up with a thousand household chores. At the same time, they have to call on all their imagination and creativity to give their child what he requires. How can you be constantly alert and available when your child is clamoring for your attention and you're utterly exhausted? All those mothers who push baby carriages along crowded city sidewalks to a dusty little park so their child can get some "fresh air" or play for a few minutes in a dirty sandbox—who worries about the quality of their life?

The city child's fate is not an individual problem, but a collective one. Nothing is done to create an urban environment for the child that is fashioned according to his scale, where he can flourish under the protection of municipal rules and regulations. In a city, the child is in constant danger. Street traffic is as hazardous as a precipice. The problems involved here are enormous, and the person who even dares to mention them risks being accused of looking

for a Utopia. However, as citizens with a certain control over how our cities are run, we should use our political power to raise fundamental questions affecting the lives of our children.

At this point I would like to make some suggestions that can be put into operation on a collective level, but I will also present some very simple propositions concerning families' individual responsibilities. I think that what is needed more than an overwhelming reorganization of our lives is the changing of certain attitudes.

What am I talking about? About taking mothers out of their isolation so they can benefit from the real solidarity around them and not be chained to their daily tasks. Parent associations

should require that apartment complexes provide space suitable for child-care centers. Because day-care centers and preschools that provide qualified personnel are still comparatively rare, it may be practical to consider simpler community solutions, which would also have the advantage of being cheaper. Mothers can get together in a place in their building complex that has been set up for child care. There each mother would be furthering her own interests as well as the interests of the entire group. And what a relief it would be for the mother of a child under three to know that she can have some free time to go shopping, run an errand, or simply relax. Certain ground rules should be established: It should always be in the same place, with the same group of children (ideally five or six of them); for each

group of children there should always be the same pairs of two parents or grandparents, each contributing a full half-day a week. This regularity and duration of presence is essential so that the faces and comportment of those in charge are not constantly changing. In this way the children will feel secure and will be provided with the continuity and sense of familiarity that they require.

For two-year-olds, such programs, under the supervision of trained professionals, are becoming easier to find. Part-time care is also available in toddler or "two-year-old" programs which offer a regular plan of activities supervised by a teacher trained especially to work with two-year-olds. Such programs give the nonworking mother a daily respite from parenting without the expectation that she must at some time assume the responsibility for the entire group (as in play groups in a parent's home). Meetings for the parents of children in the group allow them to discuss common concerns such as toilet training, feeding, games, and toys with other parents.

The playmates of early childhood

The child benefits in several important ways from this kind of arrangement. When his mother retrieves him she will be more relaxed, and the time she devotes to him will be of better quality. He will have a place to play in without the constant restrictions that are required by city apartments. And most important, he will have playmates. For a long time, the need for contact among children of prekindergarten age was questioned. But now we know that the child cannot do without his peers. Young children help each other to make progress through emulation and confrontation, which are indispensable. Having a toy snatched away, trying to get it back, giving one away, taking someone else's, imitating something someone else is doing—all help him learn. And the child needs other children who complement him and with whom he can form attachments. From a very early age, affinities are formed. Relationships with adults are of a completely different nature from those with other children. Among peers the child—not the parent—is the role model. There is no norm to be followed, but rather examples that the child can follow or not, according to his own capabilities and desires. This is especially important for the only child, who sees his universe expanding. To find a companion, all he has to do is open his eyes—and his apartment door. On the other side of the wall, another child of the same age is also bored because he is alone, while another mother dreams of a little relief. . . . This kind of solution may take a great deal of work, and parents who attempt it

may have to combat a traditional tendency toward reserve and privacy, which is still very prevalent in cities. But why not try? It only takes a determined few to adopt and disseminate these ideas which, without being revolutionary, can widen the horizon of women and change their lives—to the greatest benefit of their children!

Living in an apartment

Living in a city usually means living in an apartment and having to raise children inside it most of the day. What can be done so the child will flourish and grow freely there, without becoming either a tyrant or a victim of his mother's mania for good housekeeping?

We have already examined several things that can be done during the motor-explosion stage

of the child who is beginning to walk. You must be resourceful! Basins of water in the center of the room are great at the day-care center, but dolls and boats and bubbles can be equally as much fun in the bathtub at home, with the added advantage that your child doesn't have to wear clothes. If you have no garden, you might try to bring nature into your home. Set up a small garden on a balcony or in a large window box that is well protected by a metal grille, and let your child play with the soil. Let your child help you pot plants or plant seeds that grow quickly, such as beans and herbs. Yes, he will occasionally make a mess, but you must learn to be tolerant. In the city, people often barely put up with children, who become a kind of outcast, as if they were too much trouble. You must learn to live with a little noise and movement, some spots on the carpet, water splashed onto the floor. For what is all that in comparison with the enormous investment in the future represented by the steady physical, motor, intellectual, and psychic progress of his first three years? A source of human capital is being constituted that will begin producing interest in a very short term.

The daily walk

The afternoon walk quickly becomes an established ritual, with mother heading through crowded city streets toward the nearest playground or park. There she does the best she can, according to the resources of her neighborhood. One word of advice: Allow the child to be as free as possible in his movements. Dress him in clothes that are all right for him to rumple and get dirty, and don't make a fuss over a little sand in his hair or a lost toy when he is playing with other children.

Roller skating is a good activity to promote from about the age of two or two-and-a-half years. Start by giving him only one skate, which he can push himself around on. After he has mastered this, he will progress to the second skate and learn to use that, too. This is an excellent exercise for developing balance. Riding toys that children propel by scooting along

are fun for the child and make the outing move a bit faster for adults.

You must also know how to take advantage of whatever is around you. For example, children who live in cities with subways can be taken for rides on them. It's an exciting experience: steps or escalators to go up and down; toll booths to go through; doors that seem to open and close by themselves; the motion of the train with its sudden starts and stops, making it hard to keep your balance. The child can learn how to hold on tightly to a pole, how to climb up on a seat and get back down again without disturbing the person next to him.

Everything that is seen, touched, or felt by the body contributes to the development and the intellectual enrichment of the small child. Trips to playgrounds with slides and swings, open sprinklers in the summer, and zoos, as well as other age-appropriate outings, make city living more fun for toddlers and parents alike. Remember, at this age all of the child's acquisitions are filtered through his body.

Then there's that most interesting trip of all, an experience all parents can share with their child: going shopping for groceries. Of course, parents who are in a hurry to make their purchases cannot turn every shopping trip into a holiday for their child. But they should at least realize that it can be one, and from time to time they should devote the trip to sharing discoveries with their child. How many interesting things there are for the child to experience, words to learn, objects to touch so their different textures can be felt! It's the game of everyday life, and every moment has its own richness and value. Sharing these moments with a small human being who sees everything with new eyes also refreshes the jaded eyes of the adult. This is living life in the present. In spite of daily routine and exhausting chores, a young mother can experience this profound new vision of each thing as a wonderful pause in her routine. Time with the child becomes time for the mother to really enjoy living.

This attitude can be cultivated anywhere, but in the city it becomes an important personal resource for coping with the inconveniences mentioned earlier. Individual and collective organization are inseparable, mutually enriching one another.

DAY CARE:
A WAY OF LIFE

"Yes, my baby is treated very well in the day-care center. When I pick her up in the evening, they give her back to me all clean—I don't ever have to bathe her anymore. And they even give me her last bottle all made up, ready to take home. Personally, I'd rather have more to do for her myself. . . ."

The young woman quoted above has revealed her ambivalence. On the one hand, she is happy to have found a place for her child in a good day-care center. And how can she really complain when such places are still so rare and sought-after? On the other hand, she feels supplanted.

But what is preventing her from fixing her child another bottle, or giving her another bath?

Obviously, nothing. She just has to dare—dare to be the mother. Dare to admit to the head of the center the discomfort that she feels. It's hard to go back to work and leave your baby in the care of others. But the people who work in day-care centers know this; the director will understand, and she will be able to establish a dialogue with the mother that should help make her feel more comfortable with the situation. This woman is clearly unhappy about being separated from her child. If things begin this way, there is no doubt that the child too will have trouble adapting to the situation.

The "right age" for day care

Day care is a way of life in an environment created especially for the child, adapted to her needs. But it is important that the separation from her parents be made gently and gradually. And there are periods when such a separation is definitely to be avoided. During the first three months, if the child is being breast-fed, mother and child are inseparable. And for a multitude of emotional and psychological reasons, breast-feeding is strongly recommended today. Nursing one's baby is an irreplaceable experience, a pleasure shared by mother and child. Exhaustion, which is often invoked by mothers as an argument against it, can be alleviated if the father is willing to share the household chores. Many do today, and the

special bond that is formed between the parents and the child will be enhanced and will permit better adaptation by the child when part of her care is finally entrusted to someone else. Even when a mother is incapable of breast-feeding, or chooses not to, bottle-feeding her child herself, particularly during the first three months, can be a very important and binding experience which she will not want to give up lightly.

There is another age at which placing your child in a day-care center can be very disturbing for her: eight to eighteen months. At that age the child recognizes the person who is taking care of her, and an emotional bond will have been formed. She will not easily accept any change, especially being placed suddenly in a group situation.

The choice of child care is a very serious matter, and there are various possibilities available today: care in the home or outside it; a private nanny or a housekeeper; or a regular day-care center or preschool. Let me state

clearly that there is no form of day care that is intrinsically good or bad. There are good nannies and not-so-good nannies, good centers and not-so-good centers—just as there are good mothers and not-so-good mothers. It is a matter of people and how they relate to each other. The mother mentioned above, who was ambivalent about giving up the sole responsibility for her child's care, probably would have felt equally ambivalent about a private nanny, fearing the child's inevitable attachment to her. The ideal situation would be for every mother to have a choice, to have the option of prolonging maternity leave, or going back to work part-time. It is in this area that family legislation is needed.

Many women are perfectly happy to resume their careers almost immediately after childbirth. This is their right and they should not feel guilty about it. People must realize that a mother's state of mind is inevitably reflected onto her child, who will mirror her content or discontent, and that it is usually preferable to have a satisfied mother at home with her child

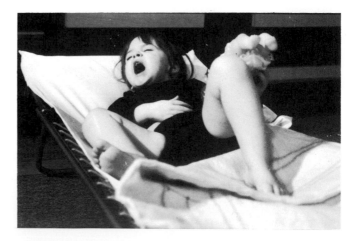

part-time than an unsatisfied mother at home full-time.

All these matters, and many others, are being discussed in day-care centers and preschools today, for these institutions are in a process of evolution. Many of them are trying to gradually integrate anything that can contribute to the well-being of the children and their parents, basing all changes on sound psychological principles. The relationship that is established with parents is an essential part of this. Thus, the newcomer is not delivered to the center or

nursery like a package left at the post office. Before the mother leaves the child in the center for an entire day, she goes there and takes care of her for a few days, feeding her herself and meeting the staff. This gives the child time to get used to other faces, other activities, and new surroundings with the mother still there. In this way day care becomes not a sudden plunge into the unknown, but a precious opportunity for the child to make many new discoveries.

In spite of all your careful preparations, there are some children who stubbornly rebel against entering into a group situation. It is better not to force them. After all, some adults can't stand communal life, either. You must try to find another form of child care, even if it is not easy to do. This is the price to be paid, during this period of establishing foundations, for the future equilibrium of your special child.

However, when parents have no choice because they cannot afford private care in their own home, or because both parents must work, or because the parent is a single parent,

care should be taken to ensure the best possible entry into the day-care center. Parents should discuss any problems with the center's director and should not feel rushed to leave their child at the center before they and the child are ready.

It's not enough to like children

The day nursery or day-care center is first of all a team, with its director, child-care specialist, teachers, and auxiliary staff. It is these people—through the attention they lavish on the children and their love for their job—who determine the quality and the ambiance of the institution. Such centers are becoming more and more open to new ideas and experiences, as well as to the children's families. They hold meetings among centers where the different staffs can share their problems. Many fruitful innovations have begun with such meetings—for example, the "mainstreaming" of handicapped children. Today many day-care centers will accept deaf, blind, or exceptional children. Not only do they adapt well, but their

presence allows the other children to develop rich and unexpected ways of relating to one another.

Where once there was little in the way of licensing or accreditation for people who worked with children under age three, today there are a growing number of programs specifically designed to ensure the level of expertise of the child-care teacher and the quality of experience for the children. Yet much of the training of child-care personnel takes place on the job, for it is a never-ending process. The idea that liking children and being female is sufficient preparation for taking care of them is nonsense. In fact, taking care of other people's children, giving each one the emotional support she needs, without becoming overly attached or forgetting that the child has a

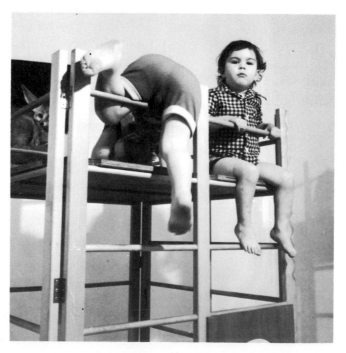

mother, is a delicate job, perhaps one of the most difficult there is. Everything is a question of subtleties in this profession where it is' all too easy to do things to extremes: showing too much attachment or being too cold; being possessive toward the child and cold toward the mother or, conversely, being too indifferent; playing favorites.

The person who "loves children" and wants to go into this profession will have to learn not just the many ways of diapering a baby and preparing a bottle, but also how to become aware of the emotional importance of her role.

A privileged environment

The preschool or day-care center is a world created especially for the child. The experiences the child can have there are complementary to those she has at home; they are special and cannot be obtained elsewhere. A notable one is group life, which brings constant stimulation. The role models here are no longer adults, but playmates. The skill in piling up

blocks or the overcoming of an obstacle that one child has just accomplished will be imitated by another—without her being forced to do it. In a day-care center you can witness the first steps of a nine-month-old child or those of another child who is seventeen months old. No one is surprised by this; it was simply time for each child to start walking.

Successful group life also brings about the unfolding of the children's personalities. The child who is a born leader, the child who is always getting into fights, the passive or the fearful child, are there side by side, and it is up to the staff to keep an eye on them, evaluating the possible risks they pose to the other children. But risks are reduced to a minimum in an environment where everything is set up for children, so one rarely hears those admonitions that are so common in the home: "Be

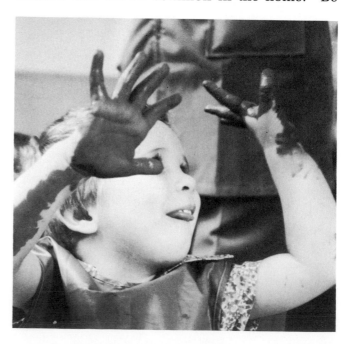

careful," "Don't touch!"—and so on.

What is occasionally missing is the richness of actual domestic life, the sessions in the kitchen where the child can help prepare meals. Because of their size, kitchens in child-care centers are not usually part of the child's territory. On the other hand, the older children can already practice making dough; baking is one of the many activities possible in this place that is so encouraging of creativity.

Many "delicious" experiences are impossible

in the home. For example, in your home could you let your child walk barefoot in paint and then make pictures with her feet on papers placed on the floor? Or even paint directly with hands that are paint-smeared up to the elbows? The availability of these opportunities sometimes frightens parents, who think they will see these "creative innovations" practiced in the home, too! But it is extremely rare that the child herself does not distinguish between what is possible and permissible in the center or school and what is possible at home. As always, it's a question of the pact you make with your child: "Here at home there's no place for you to do it. You can play another game." Parents who run out of ideas and don't know how to keep their child busy on a Sunday can get ideas from games played at the day-care center. Moreover, the child herself might think of these. But certainly time spent in a day-care center does not exempt parents from the obligation to spend time with their child in the evening. The child needs and expects this contact with them for the emotional fulfillment of

her day. The amount of time spent is less important than its quality. No matter how exhausted the mother is after her day at work, she must make this time! It will bring relaxation, and pleasure shared with her child, who will grow up all too quickly—and the time will be gone forever.

At home and at the day-care center: the same child

The daily separation and the distinction made

between what is allowed and what is forbidden—won't they cause conflict in the child and split her into two children, the home child and the nursery child? There is indeed a risk, and this is one of the problems being studied by day-care centers. The solution is a friendly working relationship to be established between parents and staff. The child is not a package to be left in the morning and picked up again each evening. Many day-care centers and preschools now spread out their arrival and pick-up times. This allows the parents to talk with the staff, to give and receive information concerning the child's activities: her minor bouts of illness in the night, her conduct during the day, how much progress she's made, her first steps, her first tooth—all of which can be discussed in the child's presence, serving to reunite the home child with the nursery child. But since the life chosen for her does give her two distinct settings, and does not allow her to live under the care of just one person, it is very important that she can feel the *accord* that exists between the two sets of people who care for her, and that there be a kind of unity in her life. This will avoid the child's having to readapt to the center every Monday after having spent the weekend at home.

The more developed the relationship between parents and staff, the more unity the child will perceive in her life. There are often parent–staff discussion groups, and some of these have even led to parent–staff encounter groups. This is an excellent way to bring about a synthesis, in the interests of the child and of everyone else, too.

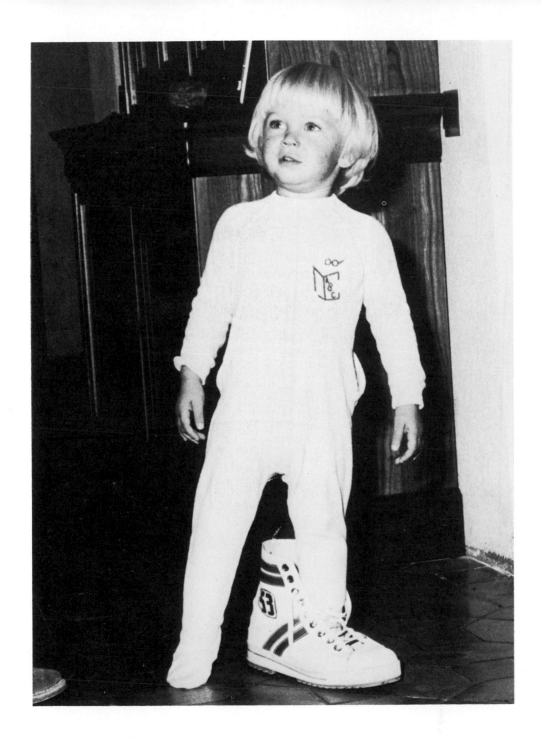

Preparing for the next stage

One fine day the time comes for the child to leave the nursery school and day-care center for kindergarten. But is it really a fine day? It means living through another passage, another separation. Preschools and day-care centers can effectively prepare the child for this transition. Many directors of these programs have contacts with kindergarten teachers and the principals of their schools, and can take their oldest children to visit their future school.

If she has adapted well to preschool life, if she was happy there, if she made progress each day, exploring new possibilities, the child will be well prepared to enter another group.

Another stage is about to begin for her and for her parents.

THE CHILD WITH
A HANDICAP

A child like any other? Not exactly, but a child *among others*. How careful we must be of our speech when we bring up the question of the child who has a handicap. Here every word is important, charged with a message of suffering or of hope. Many children from birth or early infancy manifest a handicap: Down's syndrome, blindness, deafness, cerebral palsy, and so on. Here we must remember that we are not dealing with a handicapped miniature adult whom society has difficulty accepting and therefore integrating into itself. We are dealing with a child who has a handicap, but above all we are dealing with a *child*.

The nuance is important, because it determines the way in which his parents will look at such a child, and the way we will contribute by our attitude and by our vocabulary to helping a suffering family—or plunging it even farther into desperate solitude.

Two case histories

I should like to relate two episodes, fundamentally alike and yet so very different, of two mothers who each gave birth to a daughter with Down's syndrome.

The first mother already had three children. The birth of her daughter was difficult and she had been anesthetized. As she awoke, a voice she could not identify was asking her, "Do you know what Down's syndrome is? Mongolism? Your daughter has all the symptoms of it. The pediatrician will confirm it for you later." The voice withdrew, and another voice started up: "What's she doing? . . . She's crying!"

Anonymous voices, with no one stepping forward to offer comfort. The mother was left alone in her hospital room. "After two days they brought me my baby. But is it really *my* baby? No! It's the mongoloid!"

The other young woman gave birth in a clinic noted for its innovative attitude toward childbirth. She had prepared for the occasion as though it were a holiday. Her husband was there and took the child to bathe it. The mother sensed something strange in the atmosphere of

the room. Then the father said, "She has a funny face!" and when the baby, having been immersed in water, opened her eyes, the mother saw and understood. "Then," she said, "I cried, I howled, I said *no!*" The midwife held her and comforted her. When she returned to her room, she could cry as much as she wanted to. She sensed that not far from her were watchful and discreet people, ready to step in if needed. "They were *there,*" she said. When her daughter was brought to her to be nursed, she accepted her and put her to her breast. "When she began to suck, she was *my child!*"

These two true stories illustrate two different attitudes, two reactions that are exaggerated almost to the point of caricature: massive rejection and instinctive acceptance. In the first case, the mother's reaction to her child was completely upsetting; in the other, it bestowed a promise of comfort and help for the coming battle.

The look that kills

The mother of a handicapped child will often have to wage a battle against hostile looks from people and the cruelty of their prejudices. There is the look that turns away, that does not see, that passes over your head. But there is also a look that sees and understands. Has our society finally begun to understand the suffering of these parents, or at least to show the respect of silence? How many mothers have been hurt by remarks overheard in the street, by people saying, "If I were in her place, I'd . . ." You can never put yourself in someone else's place. As for stories of heredity and genetic defects—how many idiocies are still told in their name, even today! It can never be stated enough: Don't judge, because you have neither the right nor the capacity to do so.

Even doctors don't always find the right words. A mother went to see a specialist about her six-month-old baby, who was worrying her. "I arrived with *my child* whose arms were a bit stiff. I left carrying a *cerebral palsy victim*. To me he was no longer the same child."

There are words that bear an indelible stamp, words that kill hope and zest for life.

The right to be different

But the handicap is quite real, and the situation must be faced—idealizing it serves no purpose whatsoever. This child is not like every other child. He will never go beyond certain thresholds, but each one will cross his own appropriate thresholds. Yes, his parents' love and the help that is given him may increase his chances of progress. But it is his mother who

has to be helped first. She must feel that she is heard and understood. This child is not the marvelous baby she had imagined and dreamed about. It's true that the situation isn't fair. And if she rebels, it is within her rights to do so. Yet she will also receive much joy from her child, joy she must discover for herself. Telling her about it would be completely inappropriate.

What can be said to parents who have learned that their child will not be like other children? We know that the situation seems impossible to accept, but there are groups that can help sustain them on the long road from revelation to recognition and acceptance of their special child.[1]

1. For advice about children with mental, physical, emotional, and learning handicaps and information about existing programs for these children, contact:

Closer Look
The National Information Center for the
Handicapped
NEA Building
1201 16th Street, N.W.
Washington, D.C. 20036
(202) 833-4160

Ever since day-care centers and schools have begun admitting handicapped children, the other children themselves have begun teaching adults a lesson. Among themselves, before the social molds have been set, young children accept each other as they are and help one another. The handicapped child is integrated into the group without being overprotected. Stephanie, a little girl with motor difficulties, is drawing alongside the other children in a kindergarten class. She drops her felt-tipped pen. A gallant little boy rushes over and picks it up for her. A few minutes later, the little minx drops it again, on purpose, and the same little boy comes rushing up to get it. But a third child intervenes: "Hey, she's pulling your leg!" The limit is clearly perceived; and in this way the children help structure one another's lives.

"What are you going to be when you grow up?" a little boy was asked. "I'm going to be a baker." "Why?" "So my little brother can put the cherries on the cakes." A touching expression of brotherly love: the older boy knew that

his younger brother, who was handicapped, was capable of performing that task. He created a job for him!

For each person, a way of life

All parents need to be supported, listened to, and guided when their child presents a problem, whatever it may be. Without dwelling here on this topic (which will be the subject of my next book, *A Child Among Others*), I will mention a few specific attitudes that can be adopted when dealing with a handicapped child.

The handicapped child has his own rhythm

You must know the limits of urging your child on. But don't let him isolate himself or remain too inactive either. From the moment a mother learns how to observe her child, she can introduce activities (in the form of games) that suit

his abilities. She will also recognize his unique personality, for he too can be timid or reckless, happy or sad, good-natured or sulky— but never truly wretched, if he feels he is loved as he is.

The blind child

If blindness seems to be an isolated and isolating handicap, the blind child must be brought up as normally as possible. Every action must be verbalized for him, all gestures must be preceded by words, and you must always forewarn him of what you are going to do: "I'm

going to pick you up," "I'm going to give you your bottle now," "I'm going to wash your hands," "You hear the door? It's Daddy," and so forth.

All children need some routine, but the blind child needs more than others. Nevertheless, he must slowly become accustomed, from very early on, to coping with new situations by himself. You should not remove every obstacle from his path, because there will always be new ones, and he will have to learn to deal with them alone.

The blind child's perceptions of the world of sound, touch, and smell are intensified, and there are many games that will allow you to capitalize on this.

But above all, you must *look* at the blind child. He perceives the communication established by another person's look, he "feels" you

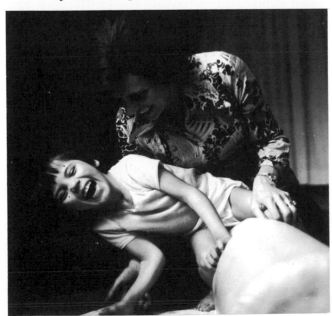

looking at him. Looking at him when you speak to him will teach him what one mother said to her little boy: "Look with your ears!" In the same way he perceives, more than any other, the feelings that cut across a silence, a gesture, the way he is carried or caressed. The love that surrounds him and the education he receives during his early years will resound throughout the rest of his life.

The child with cerebral palsy

Parents play an important role during the first months of this child's life, and they will need guidance as they attempt to adapt their daily lives to his special needs.

The parents of children with cerebral palsy have a difficult role to play. They will have to make their child understand why he is the way he is, so that eventually he can adjust. They must explain his situation to him in clear, precise, and even scientific terms. This should be done very early on, even if they think he is too young to understand. This is one of the hardest things parents can face, for they see their child suffering in body, heart, and spirit.

But we must never forget that these children *are children*, that they must have the right to be happy, to have friends, to play, to relax.

Their daily life should not be turned into one long therapy session. Swimming should be offered them for the pleasure of water, horseback riding for the joy of mastering an animal.

Society should allow these children the rights of childhood, including the right to be different and to know it.

LIVING IN
THE PRESENT

Three years in a lifetime. It's not much when you look back on it, but it's a lot while you're living it. Past time has a subjective value. The three foundation years that will turn the child into a well-balanced girl or boy or a "problem child" are experienced by parents (especially mothers) with particular intensity. They experience the great joys of these years, and they manage to put up with the exhaustion.

The arrival of a child—especially the first child—changes the rhythm of life. The attention the young woman and young man lavished on one another has converged in a new focal point that unites them more—even as it takes them away from each other. The place the baby takes in their lives grows daily. How

can they strike the right balance, and give the child all the opportunity she needs to flourish, without letting her become the only center of interest in their lives?

In the preceding pages I endeavored to show the way. The advice I offered comes down to a few simple but essential suggestions:

—Know that all of the child's acquisitions are filtered through her body and her developing senses. That is why I have concentrated on motor—or, more specifically, psychomotor—development.

—Remember that the general educational approach advised always concentrates on the *specific child*. Parents are dealing with a human being who is and will always remain herself, and not with theoretical principles. The

same education can bring about different results, according to each child's personal evolution. Every human being is unique.

—Always bear in mind the concept of the pact. This concept will have to be modified as the child grows and new possibilities become open to her, but it must remain in force. No "martyred mother" or "child tyrant."

—Finally, know that these years will pass all too quickly. This fantastic treasure that parents are responsible for, the development, progress, and equilibrium of a human being, body and mind together—all this is going to be played out in so short a time! These are years that will later be nostalgically recalled, but for now it is a question of *living in the present*. The mother who gave up working as well as the one who has the child cared for, the one who has a lot of time and the one whose every minute is precious—they all must give their child loving and careful attention that follows the natural rhythm of her development and encourages her without ever trying to push her

or, worse, hold her back.

This constructive and fundamentally altruistic attitude is the living proof of love.

I AM!

I want to do it
I'll try
I can do it
I'll try again

*Give me
some paper
and some paint*

I have the power
of creation

The thrill
of overcoming fear

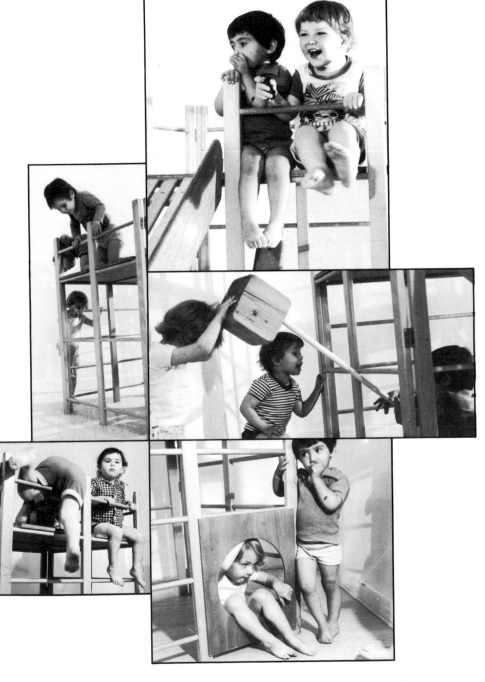

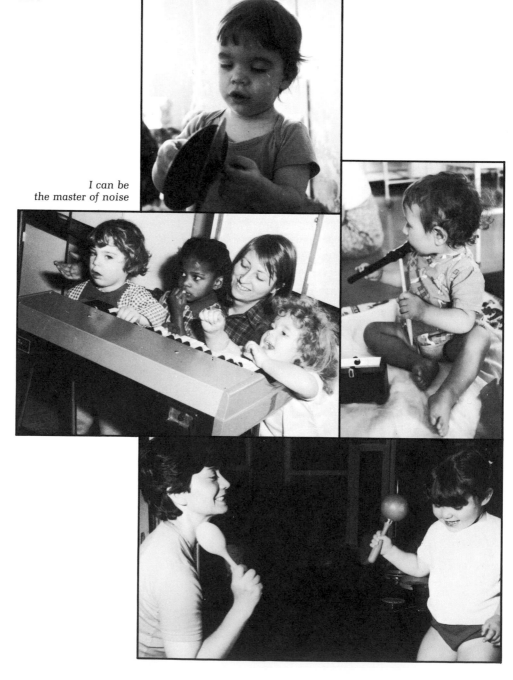

*I can be
the master of noise*

I can make
sounds
and rhythms

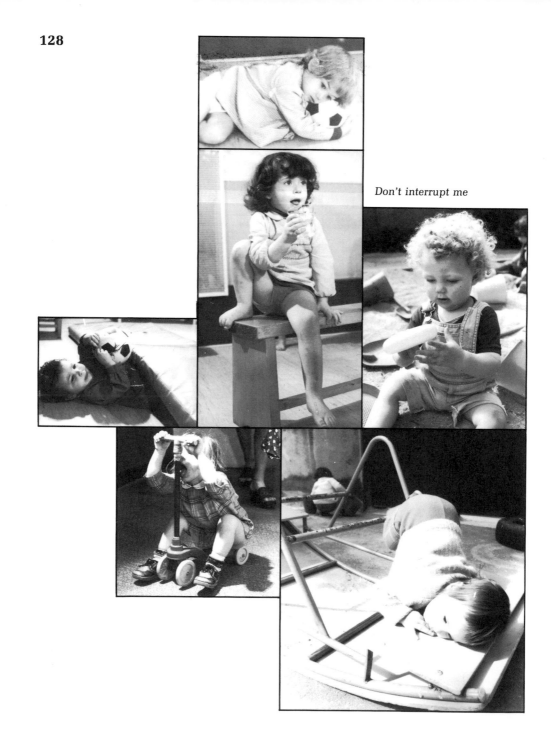

Don't interrupt me

I'm playing

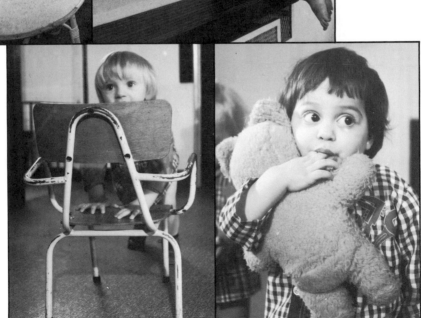

*I'm astonished
at all the things
I can do*

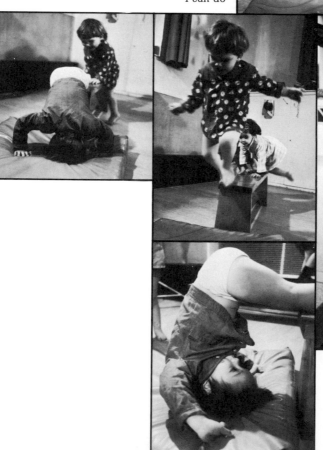

*I am the traveler,
the train and the tunnel*

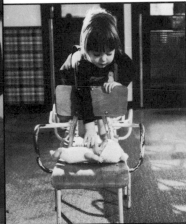

*Making my favorite
things to eat*

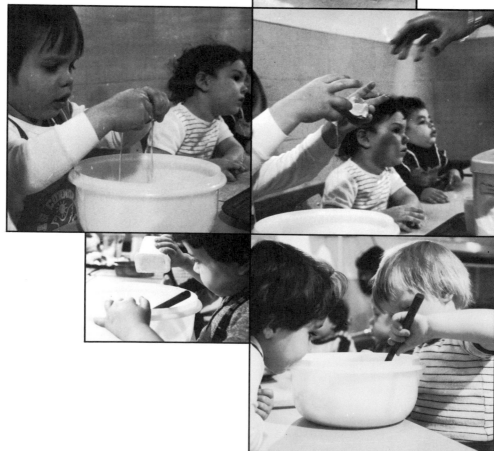

I'm the same person in all these costumes

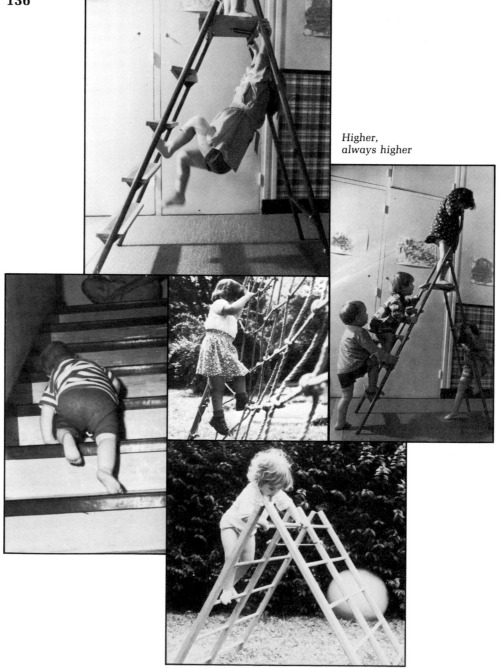

Higher,
always higher

The pleasure of
playing in water

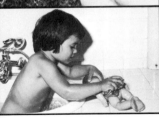

What to choose?
Should I make something
with my hands
or my feet?

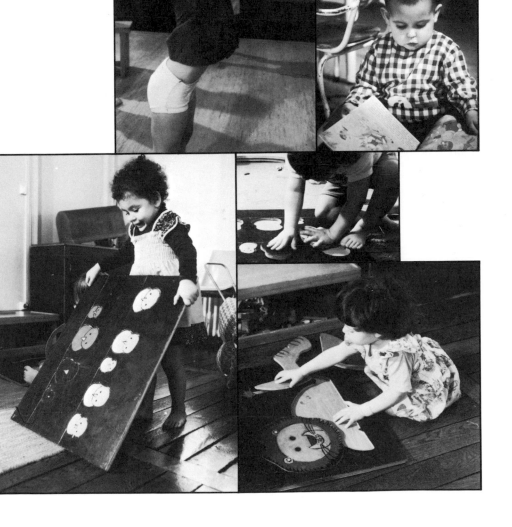

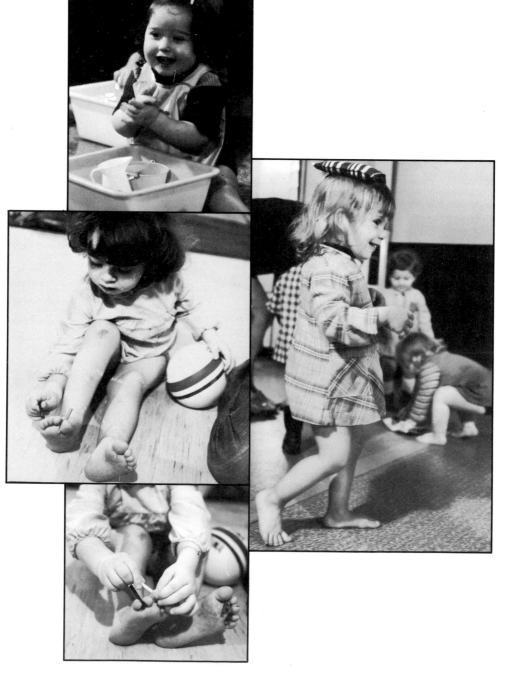

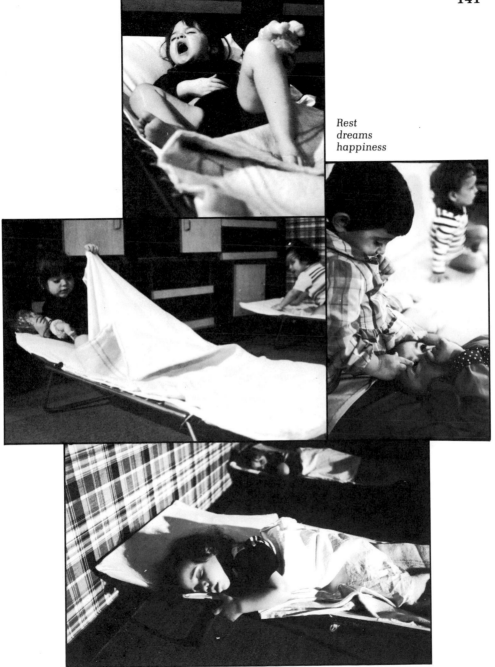

*Rest
dreams
happiness*

About the Authors

Dr. Janine Lévy, author of *The Baby Exercise Book,* is a kinesiotherapist who has created and runs a special center for infant physical development in Paris. Her work in physical rehabilitation and physical education for infants and toddlers has won the praise of doctors and child-care specialists throughout the world.

Dr. Willibald Nagler, who wrote the preface for *You and Your Toddler,* is head of the Department of Physical Medicine and Rehabilitation at New York Hospital–Cornell Medical Center.